Animals in the Wild

Panda

by Mary Hoffman

RSVP
RAINTREE
STECK-VAUGHN
PUBLISHERS
The Steck-Vaughn Company

Austin, Texas

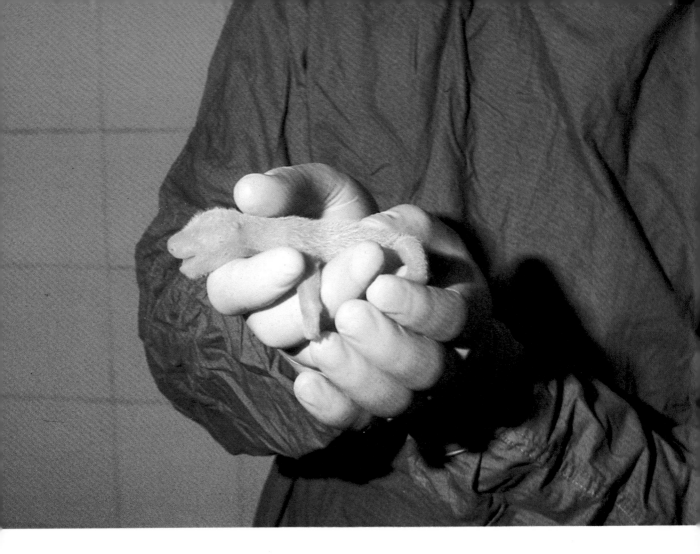

Giant pandas are not giants at birth. They weigh only two ounces. They cling tightly to their mothers for the first four days. After six weeks, their eyes open and they can hear. They crawl after four months.

Cubs weigh about twenty-five pounds when they are six months old. By then, black and white fur covers their bodies. Adult giant pandas weigh up to 300 pounds. They can be as much as five feet long.

Giant pandas come from the forests of
China and Tibet. The trees in the high

forests are bamboo. Bamboo is the
favorite food of the shy giant pandas.

For a long time, only the Chinese knew
about the giant pandas. They live in a part
of China where visitors did not go.

Then people heard about pandas and wanted to see them. No one saw a panda outside China until the 1930s.

In the wild, the giant panda spends most
of its time on the ground. It moves slowly.
But it is a good climber. Long toenails

help pandas to climb well. They climb
quickly when danger is near. Pandas also
climb up into trees to find places to sleep.

Giant pandas need to be near water. They
need water for drinking. They also swim.
Young giant pandas are very playful, and
they like to play in the water. It takes a lot
of water and food to keep a panda alive.

Giant pandas eat twenty to forty pounds of
food every day. Bamboo shoots make up a
very large part of their diet. So do other
plants. Giant pandas also eat some
animals, like fish, mice, and birds.

The giant panda has a boney knob on its paw. It works something like a thumb. It is covered by a pad. Pandas

use their claws to hold onto the bamboo
stalks when they eat. They strip away the
leaves with their teeth.

Giant pandas have white bodies with black stripes and markings. After people outside of China saw pandas in the 1930s, stuffed, toy pandas were made for children. They were popular because pandas look cute.

The Chinese call the giant panda the "white bear." Not all scientists think that the giant panda is related to bears. Some think that pandas are more closely related to raccoons.

There is another panda. It is the red panda. It is much smaller than the giant panda, and it looks like a raccoon.

The red panda has paws similar to the giant panda. Red pandas are about two feet long and weigh from six to twelve pounds.

Red pandas live near the giant pandas in Asia. They also eat bamboo. And the red panda eats other kinds of food as well.

Giant pandas are very rare, and they are being protected. The bamboo forests that feed the giant pandas are being preserved.

First Steck-Vaughn Edition 1992

First published in the United States 1984
by Raintree Publishers, A Division of Steck-Vaughn Company.

First published in the United Kingdom under the title
Animals in the Wild—Panda
by Windward, an imprint owned by W.H. Smith Ltd., St. John's
House, East Street, Leicester LE1 6NE, by arrangement with
Belitha Press Ltd.

Text and illustrations in this form © Belitha Press 1983
Text © Mary Hoffman 1983

Dedicated to Sara

Scientific Adviser: Dr. Gwynne Vevers
Picture Researcher: Stella Martin
Designer: Julian Holland

Acknowledgments are due to Bruce Coleman Ltd for all photographs in
this book with the following exceptions:
Sergio Dorantes pp. 12–13, 19, 23; Jacana Ltd Front cover, pp. 1, 8, 9, 10;
John Knight p. 2; Stella Martin Back cover, pp. 11, 14; Rex Features Ltd
pp. 3, 7.

Library of Congress number: 84-15882

Library of Congress Cataloging in Publication Data

Hoffman, Mary, 1945–
  Panda.

  (Animals in the wild)
  Summary: Shows the giant panda in its natural surroundings and
describes its life and struggles for survival.
  1. Giant panda—Juvenile literature. [1. Giant panda. 2. Pandas]
I. Title. II. Series.
QL737.C214H635   1984   599.74'443   84-15882

ISBN 0-8172-2407-6   hardcover library binding

ISBN 0-8114-6884-4   softcover binding

  6 7 8 9   95 94 93